Contemporary Hispanic Americans

EDWARD JAMES OLMOS

BY
LOUIS CARRILLO

**RAINTREE
STECK-VAUGHN**
P U B L I S H E R S
The Steck-Vaughn Company

Austin, Texas

Published by Raintree Steck-Vaughn, an imprint of Steck-Vaughn Company.
Produced by Mega-Books, Inc.
Design and Art Direction by Michaelis/Carpelis Design Associates.
Cover photo: ©John Ficara/Sygma

Library of Congress Cataloging-in-Publication Data
Carrillo, Louis.
    Edward James Olmos /by Louis Carrillo.
       p. cm. — (Contemporary Hispanic Americans)
    Includes bibliographical references (p. 47) and index.
    Summary: A biography of the man who transformed himself from a shy Chicano boy from East Los Angeles into one of the best actors of his generation.
    ISBN 0-8172-3989-8 (Hardcover)
    ISBN 0-8172-6878-2 (Softcover)
    1. Olmos, Edward James—Juvenile literature. 2. Actors—United States—Biography—Juvenile literature. 3. Hispanic-American actors—Biography—Juvenile literature. [1. Olmos, Edward James. 2. Actors and actresses 3. Hispanic Americans—Biography.]
    I. Title. II. Series.
PN2287.0438C37 1997
792'.028'.092—dc21   96-45934
[B]   CIP
                                                                    AC

Printed and bound in the United States.

1 2 3 4 5 6 7 8 9 LB 00 99 98 97 96

Photo credits: Photofest: pp. 4, 7, 8, 18, 28, 31, 34, 36, 39; B. Markel/Gamma-Liaison: p.11; ©Frederic De Lafosse/Sygma: p.12, ©1992 Herman Kokokan/Black Star: p.14; Wide World Photos, Inc.: p. 17; ©1991 Ulf Wallin/The Image Bank: p. 21; Campion-Trapper/Sygma: p. 23; Gamma-Liaison: p. 25; ©Steve Starr/Saba: p. 45; AP/Wide World Photos, Inc.: pp. 26, 33, 40; Archive Photos/Fotos International: p.43.

Contents

1 *Zoot Suit* 5

2 Ethnic Salad 10

3 Baseball and Music 16

4 Bit Parts 22

5 The Star 27

6 Race Riot 37

Important Dates 46

Glossary 47

Bibliography 47

Index 48

Chapter One

ZOOT SUIT

The audience quiets down as the theater lights dim. A spotlight slowly illuminates a huge newspaper front page that shows the zoot suit riots that took place in 1943 in Los Angeles. Suddenly a switchblade knife slits the newspaper from the top down. An actor in high-waisted, wide-legged pants with suspenders steps to the front of the stage. He puts on a long jacket with wide lapels and a wide-brimmed hat. He jams his hands into his pockets and struts forward as if to say, "This is who I am. Take it, or leave it." Luis Valdez's musical *Zoot Suit*, set in the 1940s, has begun. The theater is the Mark Taper Forum in Los Angeles, and the time is February 1978. The actor is Edward James Olmos, and the character he plays is El Pachuco.

The 1978 production of *Zoot Suit* used newspaper headlines to create a realistic stage set for the play, which is based on real events.

El Pachuco is not meant to be a real person. He is the alter ego, or the other self, of the main character, Henry Reyna. During the 1940s some young Chicano (Mexican-American) men would dress in the fashionable clothes they called zoot suits. They spoke in a mixture of English and Spanish that also included a lot of slang. They danced to Mexican *paso dobles* (marching music) and to the popular swing music of the time. They tried to appear "smooth," in control, and unconcerned. They were called *pachucos*. Like today's rock musicians, *pachucos* were romantic heroes to some and hoodlums to others.

Zoot Suit was created and performed by a theater group called *El Teatro Campesino* (The Peasants' Theater). Luis Valdez founded *El Teatro Campesino* in 1965 to support the United Farm Workers Union in their strike against the grape growers of California's Central Valley. Valdez's group designed simple sets and costumes to perform short plays in the farmworkers' camps and in the fields. They traveled in a flatbed truck and sometimes used the back of the truck as their stage. In 1967 Luis Valdez and his group wanted to aid not only the farmworkers, but all Mexican Americans. *El Teatro Campesino* decided to leave the union so they could help more people. They wrote new plays about the problems facing all Mexican Americans. The group still traveled by truck and kept their sets and costumes simple. But now their plays were seen in cities as well as in more rural areas. They

Edward James Olmos (right) in the role of El Pachuco, a gangster, in *Zoot Suit*.

performed in borrowed buildings, school auditoriums, and parks.

Luis Valdez wrote a play using real events: the Sleepy Lagoon murder of 1942, the trial of 17 young men accused of the crime, and the riots that resulted from the trial. The play combined these actual events with the music of the time, exciting dancing, and sets made up mostly of newspapers. The result produced the explosive brew called *Zoot Suit*.

Zoot Suit made Edward James Olmos a star. But he wasn't an overnight success. He had overcome shyness, studied acting, worked in theaters infested with rats and cockroaches, and supported himself with a job moving antique furniture, all with the goal of becoming a serious actor. In the process Eddie Olmos, a shy Chicano kid from East Los Angeles, transformed himself into one of the best actors of his generation. He was the first Chicano actor to play realistic Chicano characters in stories about the Chicano experience in the United States.

There had always been Hispanic actors in Hollywood. During the silent film era, about 1910 to 1927, some of the brightest stars had been Hispanic: Dolores Del Rio, Ricardo Cortez, and Ramon Novarro. Then in the early sound era of film, about 1927 to 1935, Gilbert Roland, Leo Carrillo, and Lupe Velez were important names. Later on came Anthony Quinn and Ricardo Montalban. These actors played Latin lovers, exotics (unusual

The cast of the 1995 film, *My Family*, which starred Edward James Olmos (bottom left) and Jimmy Smits (standing in back).

people from faraway lands), sidekicks, or comics. They supported the stars, who were mainly white. The lives and stories of real Hispanic people living in the United States were hardly ever looked at. Even if they appeared in a movie, Hispanic life and culture were never central to the story.

After Edward James Olmos's success in *Zoot Suit*, he looked for stories that would reflect his experiences and those of the people he knew. This led him to movies such as *The Ballad of Gregorio Cortez* (1983), *Stand and Deliver* (1987), *American Me* (1992), and *My Family* (1995). Chicanos watching those films could finally see their lives reflected on the screen. They weren't always happy with what they saw, but at least the experiences shown on the screen were their experiences. These stories were about emigrating to Los Angeles from Mexico, having to learn English, struggling to survive and raise a family, and enduring racial prejudice.

Because of films like these, millions of Hispanic Americans feel a new pride in their culture and their language. They have a new hero in Edward James Olmos, who isn't a Latin lover, an exotic, a sidekick, or a comic, but a talented actor. He is a part of their culture and understands and appreciates all that Hispanic Americans have to offer.

Chapter Two

ETHNIC SALAD

Edward James Olmos was born in the Boyle Heights section of East Los Angeles. Imagine you are in Boyle Heights in the 1940s. Between First Street and Indiana is a street so short it doesn't appear on many maps. It is called Cheeseborough's Lane. The houses on Cheeseborough's Lane are one-floor, rectangular wooden bungalows with porches across their fronts. The roofs are pitched slightly, forming a triangle with the top of the front wall. The front door opens directly into the living room.

Some houses and yards are neat and well-kept; others are slightly shabby. Most front yards have children's toys in them. Children play up and down the street. The adults often sit on the steps of the porches chatting, joking, and calling to a child occasionally. The families know each other. While the neighborhood is like many others in Los Angeles, it is unusual in one way. Edward James Olmos remembers

Edward James Olmos, an American of Mexican descent, fights for the human rights of all people. Here he speaks at the Housing Now March in Washington, D.C.

it as an ethnic salad. No one in the neighborhood was concerned that Mexican Americans lived next to African Americans or that Native Americans lived next door to people from Asia or Eastern Europe.

Why does Olmos call his old neighborhood an ethnic salad? He explains it this way in talking about the United States: "This country is a great salad. It's the lettuce staying the lettuce, the tomato staying the tomato, the onion staying the onion. You never lose the flavor of the Italian American, of the Native American, or of the Mexican American."

This is the neighborhood where Eddie Olmos's parents were living when Eddie was born on February 24, 1947. His father, Pedro Olmos, was born in Mexico

His lifelong commitment to his Hispanic roots won Edward James Olmos the Hispanic Heritage Award in 1992.

City, Mexico. From an early age Pedro Olmos showed a talent for business. He founded a business that distributed pharmaceuticals (medicines you buy at a drugstore) at the age of 14.

Eddie's mother, Eleanor Huizar, was an American of Mexican descent. Her grandparents had fled the Mexican Revolution of 1910 and moved to Los Angeles. During World War II, she went to Mexico City to visit her sister. There she met Pedro Olmos. He fell in love with her and made up his mind that he was going to marry her. Pedro Olmos turned over his business to one of his brothers and followed Eleanor to Los Angeles.

The young couple were married and set up house with Eleanor's grandparents in the bungalow on

Cheeseborough's Lane. A son, Peter, was born in 1944. Edward James was born in 1947, and a daughter, Esperanza, was born in 1950. It was hard for Pedro Olmos to support his growing family. He was in a new country and couldn't speak English well. He had been an important businessman in Mexico City. In Los Angeles he found work where he could, first in a slaughterhouse, then as a welder.

Edward James Olmos remembers the neighborhood fondly. Everyone knew everyone else, and they all helped each other. Mothers would ask their neighbors for small amounts of sugar, coffee, or a spice. Grocers gave their customers credit. Some grocers always had a piece of candy for children who were shopping with their parents. Sometimes Saturdays brought a special treat. Eddie's grandparents would take him to the local movie theaters. They often watched films that took place in Mexico. Eddie noticed that the people in the films were not like the people he knew.

Edward James Olmos also remembers the streets of his neighborhood as a kind of theater. The boys who lived there would try out different "roles." They would act brave and macho (manly) one day, shy and quiet the next, and something in between another day. They were trying to become accepted and find out who they were.

He hasn't done it yet, but Edward James Olmos has spoken of buying his childhood home and turning it into a museum. He wants to show the young people in the neighborhood that any goal is reachable, no matter where you come from.

The people who lived in Boyle Heights were warm and supportive of each other. But there was also gang activity in the area. When Eddie was eight, the Olmos family decided to avoid the danger of their boys becoming involved with gangs. They moved about five miles away to Montebello.

Where do Edward James Olmos's strength, drive, and ambition come from? One answer is his parents. Eddie Olmos had parents who cared about his future and well-being. Even today Edward James Olmos

Edward James Olmos uses the events in his life to enrich a role. Here he selects his projects carefully from the many scripts he receives.

credits his mother for his success. Eleanor Olmos was a devoted mother who did not stop raising children after her last child, Esperanza, was born. Eddie Olmos also had two adopted sisters and one adopted brother.

Eddie's father influenced his character in a different way. Eddie was always asking his father to tell him something about life. One day Eddie's father said, "*Mi hijo* ('my son'), you are born to die, and in between life asks but one question, 'Are you happy?'" At first young Eddie was disappointed with the answer. But years later he decided that his father's answer had been a wise one.

Shortly after the family moved to Montebello, Eddie was shocked by some unexpected news: his parents were getting a divorce.

Chapter Three

BASEBALL AND MUSIC

Eddie loved both his parents, so the divorce hurt him a lot. His relatives would always ask him, "Are you OK? Do you need anything?" Eddie just wanted to be left alone without his relatives bothering him. He would go off on his own and throw a ball up in the air and catch it, over and over again. Then he began to play sockball with the neighborhood boys. Sockball is played like baseball, except that you use a tennis ball wrapped in an old sock.

One day a neighbor was watching Eddie play ball and suggested he sign up for a neighborhood Little League team. So he joined the team. He improved his throwing and catching by practicing every day. He discovered that he liked the support and friendship of the other players and the praise they gave him when he played well. He played so well that soon he was the Golden State League batting champ.

Baseball also had an unexpected benefit for Eddie.

Edward James Olmos (second from right) with cast members of the 1991 baseball film, *Talent for the Game,* featuring real-life players Derrel Thomas (left), Willie Davis (center), and Bobby Tolan (right).

According to the divorce agreement, Eddie could see his father only for eight hours every two weeks. This was hard on the family, especially on Eddie and his father. But if Eddie was playing baseball on a Saturday afternoon, his father could go and watch him play. If the game was a doubleheader or a tripleheader, Eddie was in heaven! Sometimes his father sat in the stands on one side of the field, and his mother sat in the stands on the other side.

Baseball saved Eddie's life. He was so devastated by the breakup of his parents' marriage that he reached out for something stable, something that he liked to do, something that would keep his mind off how badly he felt. Other boys in his place might have reached out to cigarettes, alcohol, or drugs, or become a member of a gang. Instead Eddie reached out to baseball.

In the early 1960s, during the baseball off-season, minor- and major-league players played in the California Winter League. Athletes could stay in shape while scouts watched promising young minor-leaguers play in real games.

During the Winter League season, major-league stars sometimes traveled to neighborhood parks and gave baseball clinics. They would play with and coach the neighborhood teams. One clinic was held in Montebello, and Ed Roebuck, a star Los Angeles Dodgers pitcher, chose Eddie Olmos to catch for him. This was a great honor for the young boy, who had only recently joined the Little League.

When he was about 13, Eddie Olmos became

Ed Roebuck, Los Angeles Dodgers pitcher, chose Eddie Olmos to catch for him when he coached neighborhood teams in Los Angeles.

interested in something else that he would devote himself to and practice until he had mastered it. That something was music. He loved the music of Little Richard, James Brown, and the other early stars of rock and roll. Using a borrowed guitar, Eddie would imitate his favorite singers for hours. He studied their performances and practiced the way they sang, the way they played the guitar, and even the way they moved. This made Eddie a popular guest at parties. About his singing Eddie has said, "I was the worst. However, I worked at it, like I had with baseball, until I developed a kind of style."

Eddie's father had always been a good dancer. After the divorce Eddie and his brother and sister would visit their father in his small apartment. Eddie has described how his father would put on music and, there in his small kitchen, would change from a shy and unhappy man to the king of the dance floor. Eddie remembers his father dancing all the popular dances of the 1940s and the 1950s: the two-step, the jitterbug, the mambo, and the cha-cha. His father would dance with Eddie, then with his sister Esperanza. Then Eddie and Esperanza would dance together. His father never bragged about his dancing, but Eddie knew that his father was secretly proud of himself and proud of his children's dancing abilities. Years later when he was trying out for *Zoot Suit,* Eddie would have reason to be thankful for what his father had taught him.

Throughout high school Eddie kept up his interest

in music. Before he graduated from Montebello High School, he formed a band called The Pacific Ocean with Denny Dias and Hirth Martinez, both guitarists. The band played the music of Chuck Berry, Little Richard, Fats Domino, Bobby "Blue" Bland, and Howlin' Wolf. Later the band added a folk-country sound to the soul/blues/jazz/rock music that it played. After graduating from high school in 1964, Eddie and his band began to play at Gazzarri's, a nightclub on the Sunset Strip. The Sunset Strip is a part of Sunset Boulevard in Hollywood that has a lot of nightclubs and restaurants. The band was billed as "Eddie James and The Pacific Ocean."

Gazzarri's allowed Eddie to improve as a performer. He sang and danced. He learned how to be an emcee (master of ceremonies, or a person who introduces performers). He made people laugh. He learned how to "read" an audience, that is, how to respond to the way the audience is feeling. During this time he was also attending East Los Angeles College (from 1964 to 1966) and Cal State Los Angeles (from 1966 to 1968). It wasn't easy to be in classes during the day, perform at Gazzarri's at night, and keep up with studying and assignments. However, Eddie used the same determination and discipline that he had applied to baseball and music to help him succeed. He explains, "I used to bring my books to the gigs, and between sets I'd do my homework." (A gig is what many musicians call the jobs they get performing.

Eddie James and The Pacific Ocean, Edward James Olmos's band, played at clubs similar to this one, in Los Angeles.

The music that a band plays at one time without taking a break is called a set.)

By 1968 The Pacific Ocean was playing at an important new club located in an old warehouse. It was called The Factory. Many famous people came to the club, including Judy Garland, Frank Sinatra, and Mick Jagger. Many people would have been satisfied with this success, but Eddie Olmos felt that something was missing. He had conquered baseball and music. What would he conquer next?

BIT PARTS

In 1966, his first year at Cal State Los Angeles, Eddie Olmos decided to take a drama course. Eddie wanted to learn how to be comfortable onstage. He had never had a great talent for singing, and he found that he liked to express his feelings by speaking lines instead of singing them. That's when he knew that someday he would be an actor.

While Eddie was playing at Gazzarri's one night in 1967, a beautiful young woman named Kaija (KI-ya) Keel walked in with a girlfriend who knew Eddie. When Eddie and Kaija were introduced, they instantly became friends. They began to see a lot of each other and knew they were becoming closer and developing a serious relationship. Soon it was time to meet the young woman's family.

Kaija is the daughter of the movie star Howard Keel. The Keels lived in a mansion in Beverly Hills, California. Kaija's parents were not happy about their daughter's new boyfriend—he was not what they had expected. He had hair down to his waist, was a rock-and-roll singer, and had no money.

The first dinner with Kaija's family was awkward. Eddie remembers being served an artichoke, a food he had never eaten before. He peeled it all before he realized that he was supposed to eat the thick part of each leaf.

Despite these difficulties, the young couple were married in 1971. They knew that the change from rock-and-roll singer to aspiring actor was going to be difficult. They had to budget their money carefully. They lived simply. Two boys were born to them, Mico and Bodie. The name Mico comes from the Spanish *mi hijo* (my son). To support his family, Eddie

Outside the 1989 Academy Award ceremony in Los Angeles are Edward James Olmos, his wife Kaija, and their sons Bodie and Mico.

dissolved the band and decided to start his own business. He needed a business that would leave him time for auditions and acting jobs. He remembered that the now-famous actors Gene Hackman and Dustin Hoffman used to move pianos in New York when they were acting students. So he bought the band's truck and used it to deliver antique furniture. It was hard work, but knowing that it supported his family made it easier.

In between furniture deliveries, Eddie Olmos looked for and began to get some acting jobs. He got small parts in television shows like "Kojak" and "Hawaii Five-O." He played characters like bartenders and small-time criminals. He wasn't a star yet, but he was learning how to act, and he never gave up his dream of becoming a serious actor.

In 1971 director Floyd Mutrux was casting his movie *Aloha, Bobby and Rose*. It was the story of a young mechanic who gets into a fight with a Chicano hoodlum over a game of pool. There is a knifing. The mechanic and his girlfriend run away and meet some interesting characters on the road. Floyd Mutrux gave the part of the Chicano hoodlum to Eddie Olmos. This was Eddie's first movie role. It was a small part, but Eddie made it an important one. Watching him on the screen, one believed he was dangerous; hate seemed to flash from his eyes, and his fists threw lightning punches.

Another director, Robert M. Young, was to be even

Edward James Olmos (second from right) with (from left) producer Arnold Kopelson, fellow actor Willem Dafoe, and director Robert M. Young, while filming *Triumph of the Spirit* (1989).

more important in the career of Edward James Olmos. Bob Young had a reputation for making realistic films about the many kinds of people who made up the United States. One of Young's most important films had been about African Americans, *Nothing But a Man* (1964). In 1976, when Young was casting a movie about illegal **immigration**, he met Eddie. He gave Eddie a part in the movie *Alambrista!* The title comes from *alambre,* the Spanish word for "wire." It refers to the wire fence that the immigrants had to climb over in order to reach American soil. *Alambrista!* won a gold medal at the Cannes (France) Film Festival in 1978. Eddie Olmos and Bob Young became friends and have since made several more films together.

Rock star Mick Jagger (center) visited Olmos (left) backstage after a performance of the New York production of *Zoot Suit* (1979).

Eddie was working at a small theater called the Los Angeles Actor's Theatre when he was asked to **audition** for a play called *The American Messenger Service* at the Mark Taper Forum. He auditioned, but didn't get the part. As he was leaving, a voice called out, "Hey, you!" He looked around, but he didn't see anybody. The voice called again, "Hey, you!" Finally Eddie saw a young woman seated in an office off the lobby of the theater. The woman, still sounding angry, asked, "You want to try out for a play?" When Eddie asked about the play, her response was, "Do you, or don't you?" Eddie gave up and said that, yes, he would like to try out for a play. He came back to audition and found that the play was called *Zoot Suit*.

Chapter Five

THE STAR

Zoot Suit opened at the Mark Taper Forum in Los Angeles in February of 1978. It moved to the Aquarius Theater in Hollywood that fall. It opened at the Winter Garden Theater in New York City in March of 1979. It was not a success in New York. It ran for less than two months. But *Zoot Suit* made Edward James Olmos a Broadway star. In addition he won the Los Angeles Drama Critics Circle Award, the Theater World Award, and a Tony nomination.

When *Zoot Suit* closed, Edward James Olmos was out of work once again. There were a few film offers, including the film version of *Zoot Suit*. Luis Valdez filmed *Zoot Suit* (1982) in the Aquarius Theater in Hollywood with a real audience. The power of the play was caught on film and so was the powerful performance of Edward James Olmos.

He went on to play the part of a modern wolfman in Michael Wadleigh's *Wolfen,* which was released in

A scene from *Blade Runner* (1982), which is one of Olmos's favorite movies.

1981. The part of a Native American bridgeworker who can turn into a wolf contributed to the success of the thriller and gave Edward James Olmos a chance to shine in a difficult role. Film critics felt he was convincingly possessed and wild in his Dr. Jekyll-and-Mr. Hyde-like transformations.

He also caught the attention of Ridley Scott, who was preparing to make the movie *Blade Runner.* As the evil police informant named Gaff, Olmos seemed entirely at home in Scott's vision of a twenty-first-century Los Angeles. Cars fly. Skyscrapers loom. Huge outdoor television screens beam commercials to the city. As an Angeleno of the future, Gaff is suitably multicultural. He has German blue eyes, Asian features and skin, and speaks ten languages fluently.

A few months later, Olmos turned down a lot of money and a big part in the movie *Scarface* because, "I just couldn't find myself in that movie." He also turned down a role in the television series "Hill Street Blues," because it wouldn't allow him to do other work at the same time.

The other work that was on his mind was work that was meaningful to him and to his culture. Olmos not only wanted to portray Mexican Americans in stories, he also wanted the stories to be told from the point of view of Mexican Americans.

Someone else was thinking along the same lines. **Producer** Moctesuma Esparza was planning a movie about Gregorio Cortez, a Mexican-American folk hero of western Texas. Moctesuma Esparza offered Edward James Olmos the part of Gregorio Cortez and let him choose the director. Olmos chose his close friend, director Bob Young.

At the turn of the 20th century, a cowhand named Gregorio Cortez was chased across the western Texas prairie for two weeks by Texas Rangers. He was suspected of stealing a horse, and he was accused of killing the sheriff who came to question him. He was caught, beaten, tried, and convicted. He was sentenced to a long prison term and later died in prison.

A simple misunderstanding of language was at the heart of the injustice. The English-speaking sheriff, through an interpreter, had asked Gregorio Cortez if he had traded a horse *(caballo* in Spanish*)*. Cortez replied that he had not traded a horse. He added that he had traded a mare. (A female horse is called a *yegua* in Spanish.) But neither the sheriff nor his interpreter understood that in Spanish "male horse" and "female horse" are different words. They also didn't know the Spanish word *yegua*. The sheriff and deputy accused Cortez of horse stealing. This misunderstanding led to the killing of the sheriff and to the flight of Gregorio Cortez across Texas.

The Mexican-American people of western Texas remembered the story of Gregorio Cortez. They sang about it in a song called a *corrido*. The words of *corridos* often poke fun at politicians, talk about community happenings, or tell local stories. Edward James Olmos adapted authentic Mexican music for the film and also composed some new music for it.

To prepare for the role, Edward James Olmos read about Cortez in old newspapers. He traveled to Texas to visit the location where the story took place. He tried to "get inside the skin" of Gregorio Cortez.

He made an unusual decision about the language of the film. All the characters would speak the language, English or Spanish, that they really would have spoken. No subtitles would be used. When something is translated by a character for another character, the translation is also for the audience.

This was a big change in moviemaking. There are

Edward James Olmos in a scene from *The Ballad of Gregorio Cortez*, in which he played the title character, a Mexican-American folk hero of western Texas.

three things that moviemakers do to make English-speaking audiences understand Spanish-speaking characters. One, the Spanish-speaking characters might just speak English with a Spanish accent. Two, they might say one thing in Spanish that is easy to understand, such as *sí, señor*, and then continue in perfect English. Three, their Spanish might be translated by English subtitles at the bottom of the screen.

This approach of having the actors speak in the

language the character really would have used made the film seem even more real. Olmos felt it was the best way to handle the language misunderstanding. In addition he felt it was the best way to reach bilingual audiences, the people who understood both English and Spanish.

Since the public television show "American Playhouse" had helped to finance *The Ballad of Gregorio Cortez*, the movie was shown for the first time on public television in 1982. A year later it was released in theaters. Edward James Olmos was determined to bring *The Ballad of Gregorio Cortez* to even larger audiences. Olmos traveled constantly to promote the film. He spoke to executives of large companies and persuaded them to donate copies of the film to schools, libraries, and boys' and girls' clubs. He dedicated about five years of his life and large amounts of money to *The Ballad of Gregorio Cortez*. At one point his friends organized a benefit to raise money so that Olmos could continue to travel and speak to groups about his film.

In 1984 the producer of "Miami Vice," Michael Mann, called Edward James Olmos and asked him to play the character Lieutenant Castillo, the boss of characters Sonny Crockett (played by Don Johnson) and Ricardo Tubbs (played by Phillip Michael Thomas). Olmos refused at first. He didn't want to sign an exclusive contract. An exclusive contract for a television series says that you can't do any other work while you are working on that series. After several discussions Edward James Olmos won the right to do outside work. With his usual dedication and skill, Olmos soon created an unforgettable character, the moral center of the series. He had a strong sense of right and wrong. As the boss, Castillo could persuade the police officers to do the right thing. Although Don Johnson and Philip Michael Thomas were the stars of the show, and most of the news concerning the show was about them, Edward James Olmos contributed a lot to the success of the program.

In 1985 he won a Best Supporting Actor Emmy Award for "Miami Vice." In 1986 he won a Golden

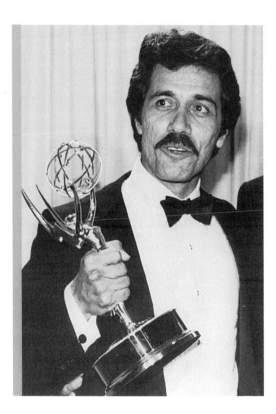

One of Edward James Olmos's proudest moments is when he received an Emmy Award for outstanding supporting actor in a drama series ("Miami Vice").

Edward James Olmos received an Oscar nomination for his portrayal of a teacher who inspired his students to excel in math in the 1987 film, *Stand and Deliver*.

Globe Award for the same program. But by that time Olmos was not as happy with the series as he once had been. He was particularly upset because the fashionable clothing and artistic sets were becoming more important to the producers than the stories. He was soon looking for another challenge.

He found his challenge in a newspaper story that led to the making of the movie *Stand and Deliver*. The newspaper article was about the success of Jaime Escalante in teaching **calculus** to a class of 18 Garfield High School students in 1982. Garfield High School served an especially poor area of East Los Angeles. The school buildings were rundown. Gang activity was common. But the area was also full of young people who knew about dedication and sacrifice, young people who were willing to be pushed to achieve. It was a challenge that Jaime Escalante met. He produced a class of math students who not only took the Educational Testing Service's advanced placement math exam but passed it with high scores.

Writers Tom Musca and Ramon Menendez had also read about Jaime Escalante's work in the newspaper. They, too, were attracted by the story and wrote a screenplay. They joined forces with Edward James Olmos, who became the coproducer and the star of the movie. Ramon Menendez directed. They filmed *Stand and Deliver* on a small budget in only six weeks.

Jaime Escalante himself didn't want to cooperate with the project at first, but Ramon Menendez persuaded him by arguing that watching the movie might inspire even more students to achieve.

Edward James Olmos prepared for the role in his usual thorough way. He studied videotapes of Escalante that had been made by Daniel Villarreal, Ramon Menendez's assistant. He gained 40 pounds. His hair was cut and combed to look like Escalante's. He wore unfashionable, baggy clothing. He shuffled, or dragged his feet as he walked.

He didn't stop with the way Escalante looked and moved. He studied the way Escalante acted with his students. Escalante often spoke strongly to his students. But his students never attacked him. Edward James Olmos wondered why. He soon discovered the

Edward James Olmos with the real-life teacher who inspired the film *Stand and Deliver,* Jaime Escalante.

secret. Escalante knew that the students thought that the situation was funny—a fat, balding, shuffling math teacher standing up to strong, young, streetwise punks. His students also knew that he loved them and that he pushed them hard because he wanted them to succeed. Edward James Olmos received an Oscar nomination for *Stand and Deliver.*

Chapter Six

RACE RIOT

Edward James Olmos now began a series of films that showed his talent for playing many different kinds of people. Olmos believes that actors become better by varying the types of characters they perform.

Saving Grace came out in 1986. In *Saving Grace* Tom Conti plays a pope who wants to get closer to the people. He escapes the Vatican and goes to an Italian hill town. There, without telling anyone who he really is, he helps the local people build an aqueduct, a pipe or channel that brings water to a place from higher ground. Edward James Olmos has a small but important part as an Italian bully and outlaw who tries to stop work on the aqueduct. It was more important for Olmos to play someone of another culture than it was to get a big part in the movie.

In *Triumph of the Spirit* (1989), Willem Dafoe plays a Jewish concentration camp prisoner from Greece, who saves himself by boxing to entertain the camp commanders. Edward James Olmos plays another prisoner, called Gypsy, who entertains the camp commanders with song, dance, comedy, and magic. His performance in this film is an example of how Olmos uses events in his own life to enrich an acting job. In this case he applied the skills he had learned at Gazzarri's on the Sunset Strip.

In *Talent for the Game* (1991), Olmos applied what he had learned at the ballpark in Montebello to this story of Virgil Sweet, a baseball scout searching for the perfect pitcher. This movie is his mother's favorite because it shows her son as he was when he was growing up.

Edward James Olmos had written music for *The Ballad of Gregorio Cortez* and had coproduced *Stand and Deliver*. He had written and directed some episodes of "Miami Vice." Always looking for new challenges or ways to expand his talents, his next film was to be one that he produced and directed.

American Me (1992) stands beside *The Ballad of Gregorio Cortez* and *Stand and Deliver* as one of the most important films Olmos has made. He coproduced the film, directed it, and starred in it. The original script was written by Floyd Mutrux in the early 1970s. It is the story of a loosely organized gang of drug dealers that was formed at Folsom State Prison in California. Olmos rewrote the script to make the gangster Santana less likable. The movie is tough to watch. We see how drugs are smuggled into prison.

Olmos (without shirt) in the prison drama, *American Me* (1992).

One brother is strangled by another. The movie ends with the sight of an innocent-faced boy of about ten calmly performing a drive-by shooting.

The movie is a warning. Edward James Olmos seems to be saying, "This is what we have come to. Do something before it's too late."

The Los Angeles Riots of April 1992 made it seem as if no one had listened to the warning. The acquittal (finding someone not guilty) of the white police officers who had beaten Rodney King started riots in Los Angeles and several other cities. Racial tensions that had been hidden suddenly erupted. Los Angeles was taken by surprise. Buildings were burned, stores were looted, and innocent people were beaten. Edward James Olmos was among the first to do something. He went on television and radio and appealed to people to stay calm. He began sweeping streets with his own broom. Soon hundreds of other people appeared on the streets with brooms in their hands. He met with Mayor Tom Bradley, California governor Pete Wilson, and other officials. He worked closely with the Rebuild LA Committee.

When he was asked by a writer for the magazine *Los*

Helping to restore calm to the streets of South Central Los Angeles, April 1992, was a way that Edward James Olmos could give back to the community.

Angeles how he got into the middle of the cleanup efforts, he explained that during the riots he had seen an African-American boy get shot right in front of him. Although bullets were flying all around, he stopped his car and ran to help. A friend of the boy's was pounding on his chest and saying, "Don't die, don't die." Another friend of the injured boy recognized the actor and said, "What are you going to do now, actor boy? This is real life, actor boy." We don't need to look any further for the reasons why Edward James Olmos works so hard to prevent violence and help so many young people. He knows that this is real life.

In the early 1990s, long separations were making Edward James Olmos's marriage difficult. Sadly Edward and Kaija Olmos decided to end their marriage in 1992. Edward James Olmos remembered the pain his own parents' divorce had caused him, and he made up his mind that he would cause as little pain as possible to his own children.

While making *Talent for the Game,* Olmos had worked with an actress named Lorraine Bracco. Their friendship grew, and they decided to get married in 1994. Each of them brought children to the marriage. Today natural and adopted children of the new family live, study, and work together easily. Olmos says, "I have an African-Jamaican son, a Swedish-Mexican son, an Italian-Armenian son, [and] a Mexican-Swedish son. And [Bracco's] daughters are English and French and English-Italian and Jewish . . . I want to have my family around me all the time." Edward James Olmos had said that Boyle Heights and the United States were like ethnic salads. Well so is his own family!

After the Los Angeles earthquake of January 1994, Edward James Olmos appeared at shelters to comfort and console the survivors. There were no cameras or microphones around. Olmos just wanted to help people cope with the **catastrophe**.

Along with his public service work, Edward James Olmos has continued to act. *A Million to Juan*, directed by Paul Rodriguez, was released in 1994. This is a **sentimental** story about a Mexican immigrant orange vendor (seller). Juan stands on street corners and sells bags of oranges from a grocery cart. One day a mysterious man in a limousine hands him a check for a million dollars. Juan finds that suddenly people are eager to give him things. All he has to do is show them the check. He doesn't even have to cash it. Edward James Olmos has a small part as a "guardian angel" dressed in a white suit. (Many people believe that guardian angels are sent to Earth from Heaven to protect human beings.)

The murder of Chico Mendes, the Brazilian activist who worked to preserve the Amazon rain forest, was the source of *The Burning Season* (1994). John Frankenheimer produced and directed the film for Home Box Office. The famous Puerto Rican actor Raul Julia played Chico Mendes. Edward James Olmos

Edward James Olmos (left) appeared with another respected Hispanic actor, the late Raul Julia, in *The Burning Season* (1994).

breathed life into his own role as Wilson Pinheiro, the union leader whose death inspired Chico Mendes to fight for the rights of Brazilian Indians.

Gregory Nava directed *My Family* (1995). Although the film was set in a Mexican-American barrio (neighborhood), it wasn't the same lifelike, gritty barrio as in *Zoot Suit* and *American Me*. It was a "prettified" barrio. Colorful people are happy and sad. They grow up, get married, and have problems. In a small part, Edward James Olmos played the family's oldest son, who becomes a writer.

Paul Williams produced and directed the thriller *Mirage* (1995). Edward James Olmos was cast as an ex-cop who is hired by an environmentalist to protect his wife who has multiple personalities. Edward James Olmos makes the ex-cop believable by using his body and his eyes to show anger, passion, panic, and the cool toughness that has become Olmos's special trademark (a style of portraying characters in a way that an actor becomes known for).

Since *Mirage* Olmos has completed *Caught*, directed by Bob Young. Maria Conchita Alonso stars with him in this modern film noir. A film noir is a film that uses light and shadow to create mood and atmosphere. *Caught* is set in Jersey City, New Jersey, and tells the story of a fish store owner, his wife, and how the tenant renting a room from them changes their lives.

Puerto Rican director Marcos Zurinaga is bringing to the screen *Death in Granada*. It is the story of the death of Federico Garcia Lorca, the Spanish poet who was mysteriously murdered in Granada in 1936. Esai Morales plays a man investigating the murder. Andy Garcia plays Garcia Lorca. Edward James Olmos shines in a supporting role.

Despite his busy life, Olmos is involved in many political and community organizations. He has continued speaking to youth groups, encouraging artists, supporting strikes and boycotts, and working for the human rights of all people everywhere. In 1994 Olmos was appointed special ambassador by UNICEF, the United Nations organization that protects children. The organization sent him to Bosnia to see how the

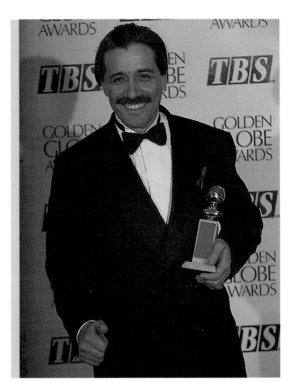

After winning a Golden Globe Award for Best Supporting Actor for his performance in *The Burning Season* (1994), Olmos poses backstage for photographers.

civil war has affected the children who are living there.

When he was a little boy, Edward James Olmos had asked his father what life was all about. He was not satisfied by his father's response that life asks, "Are you happy?" Some understanding has come with the years. Now he understands his father meant that happiness is the key to life. He suggested that it doesn't matter if you accomplish a lot or a little, if you are rich or poor, or if you are famous or unknown. Edward James Olmos's father meant the kind of happiness you feel every day when you lead a good life—that is what he believed life is all about. Olmos has come to realize that his father's answer was not a bad answer at all.

1947   Born in Los Angeles, California, on February 24.

1955   His parents are divorced.

1964   Graduates from high school. Forms the band, The Pacific Ocean.

1966   Receives degree from East Los Angeles City College.

1971   Marries Kaija Keel. Cast in first movie, *Aloha, Bobby and Rose.*

1978   Opens in play *Zoot Suit* in Los Angeles.

1982   *Zoot Suit* and *Blade Runner* movies released. *The Ballad of Gregorio Cortez* shown on public TV.

1985   Receives Best Supporting Actor Emmy for "Miami Vice."

1986   Receives Golden Globe for "Miami Vice."

1987   *Stand and Deliver* released in movie theaters.

1988   Received Academy Award nomination for *Stand and Deliver.*

1992   *American Me* released. Receives Hispanic Heritage Award. Joins the Rebuild LA Committee after the Los Angeles Riots. Divorces Kaija Keel.

1994   Acts in *The Burning Season* and *A Million to Juan.* Helps survivors of the Los Angeles earthquake. Marries Lorraine Bracco. Appointed a special ambassador by UNICEF.

Glossary

audition A tryout for a part in a TV, film, or theater production.

calculus The branch of mathematics that can help you solve problems such as how fast a spaceship needs to be going to reach the moon.

catastrophe A tragedy brought about by a natural disaster or personal misfortune.

immigration Going into a new country to live there.

producer A person who supervises or provides money for a stage production, film, or TV program.

sentimental Having thoughts, opinions, or judgments based on emotion.

Bibliography

Acker, Iris. *What Got You Where You Are Today?* New York: Distinctive Publishing Corporation, 1991.

Martinez, Elizabeth Coonrod. *Edward James Olmos: Mexican-American Actor.* Millbrook Press, 1994.

Morey, Janet, and Dunn, Wendy. *Famous Mexican Americans.* Cobblehill Books, 1989.

Index

Alambrista!, 25
Aloha, Bobby and Rose, 24
American Me, 9, 38–39, 43
American Messenger Service, The, 26

Ballad of Gregorio Cortez, The, 9, 29–32, 38
Blade Runner, 28–29
Boyle Heights, 10, 13–14, 42
Bracco, Lorraine, 41–42
Burning Season, The, 42–43, 45

Cal State Los Angeles, 20, 22
Cannes Film Festival, 25
Carrillo, Leo, 8
Caught, 44
Chicano culture, 6, 8–9, 24
Cortez, Gregorio, 29–30

East Los Angeles, California, 8, 10, 34
El Teatro Campesino (The Peasants' Theater), 6–7
Escalante, Jaime, 34–36

Garfield High School, 34

"Hawaii Five-O," 24
Huizar, Eleanor, 12, 14–15

Julia, Raul, 42–43

Keel, Kaija, 22–23, 41
"Kojak," 24

Los Angeles Actor's Theatre, 25
Los Angeles, California, 5, 12–13, 39–41
Los Angeles earthquake, 42
Los Angeles Riots of 1992, 39–41

Mendes, Chico, 42–43
Mexico City, 11–13
"Miami Vice," 32–34, 38
Million to Juan, A, 42
Mirage, 43–44
Montebello, California, 14–15, 18, 20, 38
My Family, 8–9, 43

Nothing But a Man, 25

Olmos, Bodie, 23
Olmos, Edward James
    adopted children, 41–42
    baseball, 16–18, 20–21
    birth, 10–11
    divorce from Kaija, 41
    Emmy Award, 33–34
    first movie role, 24
    growing up, 13–15
    influence of music, 19–22
    Los Angeles Drama Critics Circle Award, 27
    Los Angeles Riots of 1992, 39–41
    Oscar nomination, 34
    The Pacific Ocean, 20–21
    parents' divorce, 15–17, 41
    public service work, 42, 44
    Rebuild LA Committee, 40
    Theater World Award, 27
    Tony nomination, 27
    as writer and producer, 38
Olmos, Esperanza, 13, 15, 19
Olmos, Mico, 23
Olmos, Pedro, 11–13, 15, 17, 19, 45
Olmos, Peter, 12

Rodriguez, Paul, 42
Roebuck, Ed, 18

Saving Grace, 37
Scott, Ridley, 28
Stand and Deliver, 9, 34–36, 38

Talent for the Game, 17, 38, 41
Triumph of the Spirit, 35, 37–38

Valdez, Luis, 5–7, 27

Wolfen, 27–28

Young, Bob (Robert M.), 24–25, 29, 44

Zoot Suit, 5–7, 9, 19, 26–27, 43